MISSA
O QUAM GLORIOSUM
EST REGNUM

FOR

FOUR VOICES

BY

VICTORIA

EDITED AND ARRANGED FOR MODERN USE BY

HENRY WASHINGTON

———————

Duration of performance 25 minutes

Chester Music

PREFACE

Tomás Luis de Victoria (c. 1548-1611) left eighteen Mass compositions. His *Missa O quam gloriosum est regnum*, the best-known, was included in the First Book of Masses, published in Rome in 1583 with a dedication to King Philip II of Spain. Written in the familiar style of *Missa parodia* it derives its themes from the composer's own motet of the same title.* This superb setting of the Magnificat antiphon for the Feast of All Saints was the first item in his first publication, a book of thirty-three motets printed in 1572. A comparison of Mass and Motet reveals the surpassing skill of the Spanish master in his remodelling of the borrowed themes, giving them new life and purpose. P. Wagner in his *Geschichte der Messe* calls attention to Victoria's rare discrimination in selecting motifs most appropriate to the prayers of the Mass and to his departure from the general custom of starting each movement with a paraphrase of the same melody.

Modern editions of this Mass are not wanting. Proske first transcribed it from an original print in the Vatican Library, publishing it in his Selectus Novus Missarum. From this transcription Jacob Quadflieg prepared an excellent practical edition wherein he raised the pitch a minor third and improved the text-underlaying but retained the original note-values. A more recent Continental edition, widely circulated, falsified the melody in many places by failing to distinguish between original accidentals and editorial emendations. A copy of the original 1583 impression is preserved in the British Museum, and the present publication has been prepared direct from that source.

Missa O quam gloriosum est regnum belongs to the eighth (Hypomixolidian) mode, Tenor and Cantus adhering to the strict confines of the mode while Altus and Bassus are freer, covering a wider range. The Mass is here transposed up a minor third, the most serviceable pitch for the average SATB complement. It can be performed effectively at any pitch between this and the original, according to the vocal resources available but, in any case, the Cantus part is only suitable for treble voices.

In this edition the music text is set out unencumbered with arbitrary marks of expression. Thus, while the director is free to insert such guides to performance as he thinks expedient, singers are spared the confusion induced by his insistence on, say, a pianissimo reading when the edited score demands a contrary effect. The needs of inexperienced choirs have been met by incorporating a suggested scheme of interpretation in the *reductio partiturae*.

The sign ᶠ , a short vertical stroke placed above or below a note, is freely used in this edition with the twofold object of defending verbal rhythm against the accentual power associated with the modern bar-line, and of defining the true agogic rhythm where an original long note has been replaced by two tied notes of shorter duration. Sixteenth-century note-values have been halved to accord with later acceptance of the crochet as the normal unit of time except for the ternary rhythm of *Et incarnatus est* and *Hosanna in excelsis* where the crotchet stands for an original semibreve. The slur is used solely to denote a ligature.

The editor is responsible for underlaying the verbal text in accordance with 16th-century practice. It should be noted that a particular melodic construction often calls for elision of the final E in the word Kyrie. In such a case the E is printed in italics and is understood to be silent. An unusual feature of this Mass is the absence of a second *Agnus Dei*. At the end of the single movement is printed : *Dona nobis pacem ut supra*. This text is therefore appended to the given *miserere nobis*; but rather than repeat the polyphony the editor would prefer to reserve it for the final invocation, singing the first two invocations to an appropriate Gregorian melody.

HENRY WASHINGTON.

THE ORATORY,
    LONDON.
        March, 1958.

*Chester Edition 8787.

MISSA O QUAM GLORIOSUM EST REGNUM

KYRIE

VICTORIA
Edited by
HENRY WASHINGTON

GLORIA

CREDO

SANCTUS

BENEDICTUS

✱The original A♮ in the Cantus clashes with A♭ in the Altus. A practical alternative — if required — would be to substitute A♭ for Cantus A♮ throughout this bar.

28

AGNUS DEI

Latin Church Music of the Polyphonic Schools

A series of over 100 of the finest sacred works by the great choral composers of the Renaissance.

Masses

Giovanni Francesco Anerio (c.1567-1630)
Missa Pro Defunctis   SATB

William Byrd (1542-1623)
Mass for Three Voices   STB
Mass for Four Voices   SATB
Mass for Five Voices   SATTB

Giovanni Pierluigi da Palestrina (1525-1594)
Missa *Aeterna Christi Munera*   SATB
Missa *Assumpta est Maria*   SSATTB
Missa Brevis   SATB
Missa *Papæ Marcelli*   SATTBB

John Shepherd (?-1563)
The Western Wind Mass   SATB

Tomas Luis de Victoria (1535-1611)
Missa O *Magnum Mysterium*   SATB
Missa O *Quam Gloriosum est Regnum*   SATB

Motets

Gregorio Allegri (1582-1652)
Miserere Mei, Deus (latin text with abbellimenti)   SSSSAATBB

Giovanni Pierluigi da Palestrina (1525-1594)
Assumpta est Maria   SSATTB
Rorate Cœli   SSATB
Dum Complerentur*   SAATTB
Dum Ergo Essent* (*Dum Complerentur part II*)   SAATTB

Peter Philips (1560-1630)
Media Vita in Morte Sumus   SATTB
O Beatum et Sacrosanctum Diem   SSATB
Tibi Laus, Tibi Gloria   SSATB

Tomas Luis de Victoria (1535-1611)
Dum Complerentur*   SSATB
Dum Ergo Essent* (*Dum Complerentur part II*)   SSATB
Lauda Sion   SATB+SATB
Magnificat primi toni   SSAT+SATB
Salve Regina   SSABar+SATB

These motets are provided with both English and Latin texts.

Chester Music

Latin Church Music of the Polyphonic Schools

A series of over 100 of the finest sacred works by the great choral composers of the Renaissance.

Masses

William Byrd (1542–1623)

Mass for Three Voices	STB
Mass for Four Voices	SATB
Mass for Five Voices	SATTB

Giovanni Pierluigi da Palestrina (1525–1594)

Missa *Aeterna Christi Munera*	SATB
Missa *Assumpta est Maria*	SSATTB
Missa Brevis	SATB
Missa *Papœ Marcelli*	SATTBB

Tomás Luis de Victoria (1535–1611)

Missa O *Quam Gloriosum est Regnum*	SATB

Orlando di Lasso (1532–1594)

Justorum Animae*	SSATB

Giovanni Pierluigi da Palestrina (1525–1594)

Canite Tuba	SSATB
Rorate Cœli (*Canite Tuba part II*)	SSATB
Dum Complerentur*	SAATTB
Dum Ergo Essent* (*Dum Complerentur part II*)	SAATTB

Peter Philips (1560–1630)

Media Vita in Morte Sumus	SATTB
O Beatum et Sacrosanctum Diem	SSATB
Tibi Laus, Tibi Gloria	SSATB

Tomás Luis de Victoria (1535–1611)

Dum Complerentur*	SSATB
Dum Ergo Essent* (*Dum Complerentur part II*)	SSATB

*These motets are provided with both English and Latin texts.

U.S. $9.95

HL14034938

CH08792

CHESTER MUSIC
part of **WiseMusic**Group

EXCLUSIVELY DISTRIBUTED BY
HAL•LEONARD®

ISBN 978-0-7119-1850-4